**Practical Pre-School**

# Planning for Learning through FAIRY STORIES

Lesley Hendy

Illustrated by Cathy Hughes

## Contents

2-3 Making plans
4-7 Using the Early Learning Goals
8-9 Week 1 The Gingerbread Man
10-11 Week 2 The Elves and the Shoemaker
12-13 Week 3 Snow White and the Seven Dwarfs
14-15 Week 4 Jack and the Beanstalk
16-17 Week 5 The Princess and the Frog
18-19 Week 6 Once upon a Time
20 Bringing it all together - 'The Fairy Tale Book Day'
21 Resources
22 Collecting evidence
23 Six-week skills chart
24 Home links
Inside back cover   Parent's page

Published by Step Forward Publishing Limited
Coach House, Cross Road, Leamington Spa CV32 5PB   Tel: 01926 420046
© Step Forward Publishing Limited 2000
All rights reserved. No part of this publication may be reproduced, stored in a retrieval system, or transmitted by any means, electronic, mechanical, photocopied or otherwise, without the prior permission of the publisher.
Planning for Learning through Fairy Stories   ISBN: 1-902438-23-X

# MAKING PLANS

## WHY PLAN?

The purpose of planning is to make sure that all children enjoy a broad and balanced curriculum. All planning should be useful. Plans are working documents which you spend time preparing, but which should later repay your efforts. Try to be concise. This will help you in finding information quickly when you need it.

## LONG-TERM PLANS

Preparing a long-term plan, which maps out the curriculum during a year or even two, will help you to ensure that you are providing a variety of activities and are meeting statutory requirements of the Early Learning Goals (1999).

Your long-term plan need not be detailed. Divide the time period over which you are planning into fairly equal sections, such as half terms. Choose a topic for each section. Young children benefit from making links between the new ideas they encounter so as you select each topic, think about the time of year in which you plan to do it. A topic about stories will be suitable for any time of the year.

Although each topic will address all the learning areas, some could focus on a specific area. For example, a topic on Fairy Stories lends itself well to activities relating to Personal, Social and Emotional Development, Language and Literacy and to Creative Development. Another topic might particularly encourage the appreciation of science or mathematics. Try to make sure that you provide a variety of topics in your long-term plans.

**Autumn 1**
    Autumn

**Autumn 2**
    Christmas

**Spring 1**
    Winter

**Spring 2**
    Fairy Stories

**Summer 1**
    Toys

**Summer 2**
    Minibeasts

## MEDIUM-TERM PLANS

Medium-term plans will outline the contents of a topic in a little more detail. One way to start this process is by brainstorming on a large piece of paper. Work with your team writing down all the activities you can think of which are relevant to the topic. As you do this it may become clear that some activities go well together. Think about dividing them into themes. The topic of Fairy Stories, for example, has themes such as time, growth, reflections and change.

At this stage it is helpful to make a chart. Write the theme ideas down the side of the chart and put a different area of learning at the top of each column. Now you can insert your brainstormed ideas and will quickly see where there are gaps. As you complete the chart take account of children's earlier experiences and provide opportunities for them to progress.

Refer back to the Early Learning Goals and check that you have addressed as many different aspects of it as you can. Once all your medium-term plans are complete make sure that there are no neglected areas.

## DAY-TO-DAY PLANS

The plans you make for each day will outline aspects such as:

- resources needed;
- the way in which you might introduce activities;
- the organisation of adult help;
- size of the group;
- timing.

Identify the learning which each activity is intended to promote. Make a note of any assessments or observations

Practical Pre-School

# MAKING PLANS

## USING THE BOOK

To use this book:

- Collect or prepare suggested resources as listed on page 21.

- Read the section which outlines links to the Early Learning Goals (pages 4 - 7) and explains the rationale for the topic of Fairy Stories.

- For each weekly theme two activities are described in detail as examples to help you in your planning and preparation. Key vocabulary, questions and learning opportunities are identified.

- The skills chart on page 23 will help you to see at a glance which aspects of children's development are being addressed as a focus each week.

- As children take part in the Fairy Stories topic activities, their learning will progress. 'Collecting evidence' on page 22 explains how you might monitor children's achievements.

- Find out on page 20 how the topic can be brought together in a grand finale involving parents, children and friends.

- There is additional material to support the working partnership of families and children in the form of a 'Home links' page, and a photocopiable 'Parent's page' found at the back of the book.

It is important to appreciate that the ideas presented in this book will only be a part of your planning. Many activities which will be taking place as routine in your group may not be mentioned. For example, it is assumed that sand, dough, water, puzzles, floor toys and large-scale apparatus are part of the ongoing pre-school experience. Role-play areas, stories, rhymes and singing, and group discussion times are similarly assumed to be happening each week although they may not be used as a focus for a topic on Fairy Stories.

which you are likely to carry out. On your plans make notes of which activities were particularly successful, or any changes you would make another time.

## A FINAL NOTE

Planning should be seen as flexible. Not all groups meet every day, and not all children attend every day. Any part of the plans in this book can be used independently, stretched over a longer period or condensed to meet the needs of any group. You will almost certainly adapt the activities as children respond to them in different ways and bring their own ideas, interests and enthusiasms. Be prepared to be flexible over timing as some ideas prove more popular than others. The important thing is to ensure that the children are provided with a varied and enjoyable curriculum which meets their individual developing needs.

# USING THE EARLY LEARNING GOALS

Having decided on your topic and made your medium-term plans you can use the Early Learning Goals to highlight the key learning opportunities your activities will address. The goals are split into six areas: Personal, Social and Emotional Development, Language and Literacy, Mathematical Development, Knowledge and Understanding of the World, Physical Development and Creative Development. Do not expect each of your topics to cover every goal but your long-term plans should allow for each child to work towards all of the goals.

The following section highlights parts of the Early Learning Goals document in point form to show what children are expected to be able to do by the time they enter Year 1 in each area of learning. These points will be used throughout this book to show how activities for a topic on Fairy Stories link to these expectations. For example, Personal, Social and Emotional Development point 2 is 'be confident to try new activities, initiate ideas and speak in a familiar group'. Activities suggested which provide the opportunity for children to do this will have the reference PS2. This will enable you to see which parts of the Early Learning Goals are covered in a given week and plan for areas to be revisited and developed.

In addition you can ensure that activities offer variety in the outcomes to be encountered. Often a similar activity may be carried out to achieve different learning outcomes. For example, children can be told or read fairy stories for a variety of reasons. On page 11 an activity for making concertina books is described. It aims to encourage children to explore and enjoy books, to handle them with care in order to meet goals within Language and Literacy. At the same time, children will also be using a variety of skills which feature in the Physical Development and Creative Development goals as they make and decorate their books. It is important therefore that activities have clearly defined learning outcomes so that these may be emphasised during the activity and for recording purposes.

## PERSONAL, SOCIAL AND EMOTIONAL DEVELOPMENT (PS)

This area of learning covers important aspects of development which affect the way children learn, behave and relate to others.

By the end of the foundation stage most children will:

PS1  continue to be interested, excited and motivated to learn

PS2  be confident to try new activities, initiate ideas and speak in a familiar group

PS3  maintain attention, concentrate and sit quietly when appropriate

PS4  have a developing awareness of their own needs, views and feelings and be sensitive to the needs, views and feelings of others

PS5  have a developing respect for their own cultures and beliefs and those of other people

PS6  respond to significant experiences, showing a range of feelings when appropriate

PS7  form good relationships with adults and peers

PS8  work as a part of a group or class, taking turns and sharing fairly; understanding that there need to be agreed values and codes of behaviour for groups of people, including adults and children, to work together harmoniously

PS9  understand what is right, what is wrong and why

PS10  dress and undress independently and manage their own personal hygiene

PS11  select and use activities and resources independently

PS12  consider the consequences of their words and actions for themselves and others

PS13  understand that people have different needs, views, cultures and beliefs which need to be treated with respect

PS14  understand that they can expect others to treat their needs, views, cultures and beliefs with respect

The topic of Fairy Stories provides valuable opportunities for children to show sensitivity to their environment and the people around them, to work collaboratively and to express feelings in response to the stories they hear. This topic is especially useful in developing children's understanding of what is right and what is wrong and other moral dilemmas. As children become more aware of the characters and environments which they hear about in these well-known stories they have the chance to explore new learning and develop ideas. In addition, many of the outcomes for Personal, Social and Emotional Development will develop as a natural result of activities in other key areas. For example, when children play games within Physical Development they will also have the opportunity to further PS8.

# LANGUAGE AND LITERACY (L)

The objectives set out in the *National literacy strategy: Framework for teaching* for the reception year are in line with these goals. By the end of the foundation stage, most children will be able to:

Children will:

L1 enjoy listening to and using spoken and written language, and readily turn to it in their play and learning

L2 explore and experiment with sounds, words and texts

L3 listen with enjoyment and respond to stories, songs and other music, rhymes and poems and make up their own stories, songs, rhymes and poems

L4 use language to imagine and recreate roles and experiences

L5 use talk to organise, sequence and clarify thinking, ideas, feelings and events

L6 sustain attentive listening, responding to what they have heard by relevant comments, questions or actions

L7 interact with others, negotiating plans and activities and taking turns in conversation

L8 extend their vocabulary, exploring the meaning and sounds of new words

L9 retell narratives in the correct sequence, drawing on the language patterns of stories

L10 speak clearly and audibly with confidence and control and show awareness of the listener, for example by their use of conventions such as greetings, 'please' and 'thank you'

L11 hear and say initial and final sounds in words and short vowel sounds within words

L12 link sounds to letters, naming and sounding the letters of the alphabet

L13 read a range of familiar and common words and simple sentences independently

L14 show an understanding of the elements of stories such as main character, sequence of events and opening, and how information can be found in non-fiction texts to answer questions about where, who, why and how

L15 know that print carries meaning and, in English, is read from left to right and top to bottom

L16 attempt writing for various purposes, using features of different forms such as lists, stories and instructions

L17 write their own names, labels and captions, and begin to form sentences, sometimes using punctuation

L18 use their phonic knowledge to write simple regular words and make phonetically plausible attempts at more complex words

L19 use a pencil and hold it effectively to form recognisable letters, most of which are correctly formed

The activities suggested for the theme of Fairy Stories provide children with opportunities to respond in a variety of imaginative and role play situations. Writing letters to Jack's mother and looking at print on labels and games will help children to develop their early writing skills. Fairy Stories offers many opportunities for children to increase their vocabulary and express themselves clearly. The repeating of choruses and refrains within stories will encourage their understanding of sounds and rhymes in words.

# MATHEMATICAL DEVELOPMENT (M)

The key objectives in the *National numeracy strategy: Framework for teaching* for the reception year are in line with these goals. By the end of the foundation stage, most children will be able to:

M1 say and use number names in order in familiar contexts

M2 count reliably up to ten everyday objects

M3 recognise numerals 1 to 9

M4 use language such as 'more' or 'less', 'greater' or 'smaller', 'heavier' or 'lighter' to compare two numbers or quantities

M5 in practical activities and discussion begin to use the vocabulary involved in adding and subtracting

M6 find one more or one less than a number from one to ten

M7 begin to relate addition to combining two groups of objects and subtraction to 'taking away'

M8 talk about, recognise and recreate simple patterns

M9 use language such as 'circle' or 'bigger' to describe the shape and size of solids and flat shapes

M10 use everyday words to describe position

M11 use developing mathematical ideas and methods to solve practical problems

Well-known fairy stories are a source of interest for children and many contain numbers of people and animals, for example, the three bears, the three little pigs, the seven dwarfs and so on (M1). Some stories contain refrains which occur a number of times. The successive repeating of the chorus can reinforce counting skills, for example how many times did the Gingerbread Man say 'Run, run as fast as you can. You can't catch me, I'm the Gingerbread Man!' or the Wicked Stepmother ask her mirror, 'Mirror, mirror on the wall, Who is the fairest of them all?' ? (M1, 2). Fairy stories contain objects, animals and adventures which can be used for sorting and comparing. Stories such as 'Jack and the Beanstalk' contain comparative words such as big and little, tall and short, high and low (M4).

# KNOWLEDGE AND UNDERSTANDING OF THE WORLD (K)

By the end of the foundation stage, most children will be able to:

K1 investigate objects and materials by using all of their senses as appropriate

K2 find out about and identify some features of living things, objects and events they observe

K3 look closely at similarities, differences, patterns and change

K4 ask questions about why things happen and how things work

K5 build and construct with a wide range of objects, selecting appropriate resources and adapting their work where necessary

K6 select tools and techniques they need to shape, assemble and join the materials they are using

K7 find out about and identify the uses of everyday technology and use information and communication technology and programmable toys to support their learning

K8 find out about past and present events in their own lives, and in those of their families and other people they know

K9 observe, find out about and identify features in the place they live and the natural world

K10 begin to know about their own cultures and beliefs and those of other people

K11 find out about their environment and talk about those features they like and dislike

The topic of Fairy Stories provides opportunities to help children experience K3, 4, 8 and 11. For example, as children listen to fairy stories you will be able to talk with them about past and present events. They will also talk about the environments in which the stories occur. Many fairy stories take place in outside locations such as fields, forests, woods and near rivers, lakes and ponds (K9). When making leaves for Jack's beanstalk children will have the opportunity to practise their folding and cutting skills (K6).

## PHYSICAL DEVELOPMENT (PD)

By the end of the foundation stage most children will be able to:

PD1 move with confidence, imagination and in safety

PD2 move with control and co-ordination

PD3 show awareness of space, of themselves and of others

PD4 recognise the importance of keeping healthy and those things which contribute to this

PD5 recognise the changes that happen to their bodies when they are active

PD6 use a range of small and large equipment

PD7 travel around, under, over and through balancing and climbing equipment

PD8 handle tools, objects, construction and malleable materials safely and with increasing control

Activities such as making playdough frogs, cooking gingerbread men, and printing and painting will offer experience of PD8. Through being Jack climbing the beanstalk, jumping like frogs and finding different ways of rescuing the treasure when playing 'The Keeper of the Treasure', children can develop control and co-ordination whilst also having the opportunity to work in an imaginative way. By playing whole group games such as 'Gingerbread man tag' and 'Grandmother's Footsteps', children will become aware of space and the needs of others.

## CREATIVE DEVELOPMENT (C)

By the end of the foundation stage, most children will be able to:

C1 explore colour, texture, shape, form and space in two and three dimensions

C2 recognise and explore how sounds can be changed, sing simple songs from memory, recognise repeated sounds and sound patterns and match movements to music

C3 respond in a variety of ways to what they see, hear, smell, touch and feel

C4 use their imagination in art and design, music, dance, imaginative and role play and stories

C5 express and communicate their ideas, thoughts and feelings by using a widening range of materials, suitable tools, imaginative and role play, movement, designing and making, and a variety of songs and musical instruments

During this topic children will experience working with a variety of materials as they make playdough and gingerbread men, a row of paper dwarfs, create a large giant with different materials and make golden pom-poms to represent the princess' golden ball in the 'The Princess and the Frog' (C1, 5). By making interactive stories in the final 'Once upon a time' week they will increase their ability to use their imaginations (C4). Making up frog or gingerbread men dances will help them respond to music (C3, 4).

# Week 1

# THE GINGERBREAD MAN

## PERSONAL, SOCIAL AND EMOTIONAL DEVELOPMENT

- Encourage children to work as a group as they make and cook gingerbread men. (PS8)
- Ensure children wash their hands and keep surfaces clean as they prepare their gingerbread men. (PS10)

## LANGUAGE AND LITERACY

- Read 'The Gingerbread Man' story (by J A Rowe, North-South Paperbacks) and then ask children questions about the story. (L3)
- Show children pictures from the story and discuss how they show what is happening. (L14)
- Ask children to join in the refrain and to say it with you. (L2)

## MATHEMATICAL DEVELOPMENT

- Help children weigh the ingredients for the gingerbread men and compare the amounts of different ingredients used. Do we use more flour or more ginger in the recipe? (M4)
- Encourage the children to count how many currants will be needed for the eyes, nose and buttons on each gingerbread man. (M2)
- Draw attention to the many different animals the gingerbread man escaped from. Make a chart to show the different animals. (M4)
- Play the 'Gingerbread man journey game' (see activity opposite). (M2, 3)

## KNOWLEDGE AND UNDERSTANDING OF THE WORLD

- Discuss the different features in the landscape that the gingerbread man went through during his escape. (K3)
- Go outside and look for grass, hillocks and trees. Show them pictures of ponds to give them an idea of where the crafty fox outwitted the gingerbread man. (K2)
- In preparation for cooking gingerbread men, encourage children to describe what they see, smell and where appropriate taste. (NB Children with coeliac disease are not able to eat certain flour which contains gluten.) (K1, 2)

## PHYSICAL DEVELOPMENT

- Take children outside to run fast and slow. Can they jump over small obstacles like a gingerbread man? (PD6)
- Play 'Gingerbread man tag'. Use the fox as the chaser and the other children as gingerbread men being chased. How many can the fox eat in a given time? (PD1, 2)

## CREATIVE DEVELOPMENT

- Use playdough for rolling and cutting into gingerbread men shapes. (C1)
- Draw round a child and make a big gingerbread man that can be painted and decorated. Put him up for display. (C5)
- Make up a gingerbread man dance to some fast music.

## ACTIVITY: Making gingerbread men

**Learning opportunity:** Developing an interest in baking and understanding the need for hygiene when making things to eat.

**Early Learning Goal:** Knowledge and Understanding of the World. Children will look closely at differences and change and discuss their observations.

**Resources:** Ingredients for the biscuits; baking trays; saucepan; wooden spoons; mixing bowl; sieve; rolling pin and board; greaseproof paper; a gingerbread man cutter; spatula and wire tray.

**Organisation:** Small group.

**Key vocabulary:** Mix, stir, roll, knead, cut, bake, clean, tidy.

## WHAT TO DO:

Before children start to cook remind them to:
- tie back long hair
- wash their hands (children with eczema should wear surgical gloves)
- wear an apron or overall
- roll up long sleeves and secure them
- make sure all surfaces being used are wiped clean
- gather all the ingredients and utensils together

### Recipe for gingerbread men

Makes at least six gingerbread men (depending on size of the cutter).

**Ingredients:**

75g soft brown sugar

75g black treacle

2 teaspoons of ground ginger

$1/2$ teaspoon of cinnamon

$1/2$ teaspoon of baking powder

50g margarine or butter

250g plain flour

1 egg

currants and glacé cherries

Pre-heat the oven to 170°C (325°F/Mark 3). Melt sugar, treacle, spices and margarine/butter in the saucepan over a low heat. Remove from heat and allow to cool. Mix in baking powder. Sift flour and salt into the mixing bowl. Pour in the syrup mixture and the beaten egg. Mix together until it forms a firm dough. Knead the dough on a floured board. Leave to rest for a few minutes. (If fridge is available, wrap dough in greaseproof paper and pop in fridge for 10 minutes.)
Take dough and roll it on floured board then cut out gingerbread men using cutter. Decorate with currants for eyes, noses and buttons. Use a slice of glace cherry for mouths. Put in oven and bake for 10 minutes. Cool on wire tray.

After the cooking session is over remind children that you must turn off the oven and they must help you to:
- put away any left-over ingredients
- collect together all the dirty utensils
- wash and put away utensils
- wipe down all the work surfaces
- leave everything clean and tidy for the next group.

As the children make their gingerbread men ask open-ended questions, encouraging them to use as many senses as possible. What does the flour feel like? Do they like the smell of ginger and cinnamon?

## ACTIVITY: Gingerbread man journey game

**Learning opportunity:** Children will develop the ability to count using a game.

**Early Learning Goal:** Mathematical Development. Children will recognise and use numbers to 10 and become familiar with larger numbers.

**Resources:** A simple dice and board game.

**Organisation:** Small group working with an adult.

**Key vocabulary:** Dice, rolling, counting on, counting back.

## WHAT TO DO:

Draw a simple track on white card, marked in numbered squares up to 50. Write instructions outside the track which point at different squares such as 'Chased by the old woman - go on 3 squares'; 'Seen by the cow - go back 1 square'. Have at least six instructions.
Cut out gingerbread men shapes to act as counters. Sit with children and help them throw the dice, move their counters and read and carry out the instructions. Encourage them to count forwards and backwards as they make their moves. Point out the names of the bigger numbers as they come to them. Encourage them to play fairly.

## DISPLAY

Draw round a child and cut out a big gingerbread man. Give each child an opportunity to help paint and decorate him, then fix him to a wall or board. Put around him pictures made by individual children showing the different people and animals he met on his way. Label each person and animal to help with word and letter recognition.

# Week 2

## THE ELVES AND THE SHOEMAKER

### PERSONAL, SOCIAL AND EMOTIONAL DEVELOPMENT

- After reading the story, talk about how the elves helped the shoemaker and his wife. Discuss doing good deeds for others. (PS4)
- Look at the pictures and ask how the shoemaker and his wife helped the elves. (PS4)
- Find pictures of different sorts of shoes from around the world and discuss them. (PS5)

### LANGUAGE AND LITERACY

- After reading the story ask the children what kind of shoes they would have made the shoemaker. (L1, 3)
- Make a collection of different kinds of shoes and ask children to name them, for example, slippers, wellingtons, plimsolls. (L8)
- Make concertina books (see activity opposite)

### MATHEMATICAL DEVELOPMENT

- Cut out different kinds of shoes from catalogues and sort them into groups by colour, make, material, size. (M4, 9)
- Talk about pairs and counting in twos. (M1, 5)
- Ask children to draw around their shoes and make a pairs chart for counting practice. (M2, 8)

### KNOWLEDGE AND UNDERSTANDING OF THE WORLD

- Find pictures of shoes worn in the past such as button-up boots and riding boots. Discuss how they are different to modern shoes - no Velcro, different kinds of fastening, different materials. (K1, 8)
- Look at shoes worn indoors and those worn outdoors and observe their differences and similarities. (K3)
- Discuss the different kinds of materials used for shoes. (K1, 3)

### PHYSICAL DEVELOPMENT

- Find different ways of walking - small steps, big strides, on tiptoe and so on. (PD1, 2)
- Play 'Grandmother's Footsteps' using a small obstacle course. (PD6, 7)

### CREATIVE DEVELOPMENT

- Make up a marching dance to some marching music. (C4)
- Use percussion instruments to make different sorts of marching and walking rhythms. (C5)
- Use shoes to print patterns (see activity opposite). (C5)

## ACTIVITY: Concertina books

**Learning opportunity:** To explore books and how to make them.

**Early Learning Goal:** Language and Literacy. Children will attempt writing for various purposes, using features of different forms such as lists, stories and instructions

**Resources:** A2 paper - divided lengthways into four and folded in concertina folds.

**Organisation:** Small group with adult helper.

**Key Vocabulary:** Fold, open and close.

## WHAT TO DO:

Prepare folded sheets and cut into the shape of a shoe being careful to keep a joined edge. Unfolded it should look like a number of shoes joined together.

Tell each child that they are making a catalogue of shoes sold by the shoemaker.

Ask each child to either draw pairs of shoes or cut them from a catalogue. Stick a different pair on each page.

## ACTIVITY: Using shoe patterns for printing

**Learning opportunity:** To explore different ways of printing.

**Early Learning Goal:** Creative Development. Children will use a widening range of materials, suitable tools, instruments and other resources to express ideas and to communicate their feelings.

**Resources:** Old shoes with interesting sole patterns; a variety of papers such as sugar paper, newsprint, wallpaper, tissue paper, blotting paper; thick poster paint in different colours; brushes or rollers and a glass or perspex surface.

**Organisation:** Small groups with an adult helper.

**Key vocabulary:** Press, print, roll, brush, mix, smooth.

## WHAT TO DO:

Make a collection of worn-out shoes, either from home or from jumble sales, which have interesting patterns on the sole.

Spread colour onto the surface with either a brush or a roller.

Put a hand inside the shoe and press the shoe down onto the colour with a rolling action - starting with the heel and rolling onto the toe and transfer the shoe onto a piece of paper using the same action.

Peel off the shoe very carefully to reveal the image.

Repeat on different kinds of paper.

Use the prints for the front cover of the concertina books.

## DISPLAY

Display the concertina books and the shoe print pictures.

Make a table of different kinds of shoes and label them for children to recognise.

# Week 3

# SNOW WHITE AND THE SEVEN DWARFS

## PERSONAL, SOCIAL AND EMOTIONAL DEVELOPMENT

- Talk about different foods and the danger of eating things we do not know are safe. (PS9)
- Invite children to talk about beautiful and ugly things. Encourage children to listen carefully to the ideas of others, understanding that they may be different from their own. (PS4)

## LANGUAGE AND LITERACY

- Read the story and ask children to describe how Snow White is feeling in different parts of the story. (L6)
- Role-play the wicked stepmother and invite children to ask you questions. (L4)
- Show pictures of the different dwarfs. Can the children name them from how they look in the picture? (L5)
- Ask children to recognise their name when it is reflected in a mirror. (L17)

## MATHEMATICAL DEVELOPMENT

- Show children symmetrical and non-symmetrical objects and ask them to identify the symmetrical ones. (M8, 9)
- Make blot prints (see activity opposite).
- Count up to seven and back to one. (M2)
- Bring in a kaleidoscope for children to use and see moving symmetry. (M8)

## KNOWLEDGE AND UNDERSTANDING OF THE WORLD

- Talk about what you would find in a wood. (K2)
- Cut up an apple and look inside. (K2)
- Make a collection of shiny things and see which ones reflect. (K1, 3) Investigate mirrors (see activity opposite).

## PHYSICAL DEVELOPMENT

- Mime the seven dwarfs at work and play. (PD1, 2)
- Construct the seven dwarfs' house from large cardboard boxes. (PD8)

## CREATIVE DEVELOPMENT

- Paint portraits of the seven dwarfs showing different expressions. (C1, 5)
- Make the role-play corner into the seven dwarfs' house. (C3)
- Learn to sing the 'Hi-Ho' song from the Disney film. (C2, 4)

## ACTIVITY: Using mirrors in everyday life

**Learning opportunity:** Investigating how we use mirrors.

**Early Learning Goal:** Knowledge and Understanding of the World. Children will talk about observations and ask questions to gain information about why things happen.

**Resources:** Mirrors and reflecting objects (cover real mirrors with sticky back plastic to avoid accidents).

**Organisation:** Whole group.

**Key vocabulary:** Reflection, mirror, copy, image.

## WHAT TO DO:

Make a collection of mirrors including hand-held ones and a full-length mirror if possible. Show children the mirrors and ask what they think they could be used for, for example, brushing our hair, cleaning our teeth, painting our faces.

Encourage children to notice the way the image changes, everything is back to front.

Discuss other places where mirrors are used, for example on cars, on dangerous corners, by hairdressers.

Pass around the reflecting objects. Ask children what they see when they look at themselves in them. Is the image changed?

## ACTIVITY: Making blot prints

**Learning opportunity:** To encourage children to look at pattern and symmetry.

**Early Learning Goal:** Mathematics: recognise and recreate patterns. Creative Development: explore colour, texture, shape, form in two dimensions.

**Resources:** Thick paint in different colours (let children mix their own); big paint brushes; sugar paper.

**Organisation:** Small groups with adult helper.

**Key vocabulary:** Mix, thick, spread, brush, fold, blot, smudge.

## WHAT TO DO:

Fold a sheet of sugar paper in half and put a crease down the middle. Unfold the paper and encourage children to work on the left-hand side of the crease.

Ask them to mix two or three colours into a thick paste. With a brush tell them either to put blobs of paint on the paper or to brush paint onto the paper.

Fold the paper again and press the two halves together.

Unfold the paper to reveal the strange shape.

Discuss with the children how both sides look the same.

## DISPLAY

Make a display of mirrors. Make question labels that invite children to experiment with reflections such as 'Look in the mirror, can you touch your ear?' 'Lift your hand and ruffle your hair. What is happening in the mirror?' 'Can you find a way of looking behind you without looking round?'

# Week 4

# JACK AND THE BEANSTALK

## PERSONAL, SOCIAL AND EMOTIONAL DEVELOPMENT

- Provide opportunities for children to share and take turns when making their leaves for the display beanstalk. (PS8)
- Discuss taking other people's things. (PS9, 12)

## LANGUAGE AND LITERACY

- Read the story (by J Poole, Macdonald Young Books) and ask children to describe what the giant looked and sounded like. Write the words on a large boot-shaped piece of paper. (L1,16)
- Ask the children to remember what Jack took from the giant and in what order. (L9)
- Ask children to pretend to be Jack and help them write a note to tell his mother where he has gone. (L4, 16)

## MATHEMATICAL DEVELOPMENT

- Make groups of three. (Jack climbed the beanstalk three times, he took three things: the chicken, the money and the harp.) (M1, 11)
- Using ten beans, find ways of making them into different groups - different shape, size, colour. (M11)
- Use the leaves on the beanstalk for counting practice. (M2, 6, 7)

## KNOWLEDGE AND UNDERSTANDING OF THE WORLD

- Grow some broad bean seeds in a jar (see activity opposite). (K2, 4)

- Prepare a collection of different kinds of seeds. Discuss sameness and difference. Use words to describe the different kinds. (K3)

## PHYSICAL DEVELOPMENT

- Practise climbing the beanstalk by crawling along a gym bench or along the floor using alternating hand and leg movements. (PD6)
- Make large fruits, vegetables and foods for the giant out of playdough. (PD8)
- Play 'Keeper of the Treasure' (see activity opposite) (PD1, 2)

## CREATIVE DEVELOPMENT

- Paint and cut out giant leaves to make a beanstalk that can be displayed going right up the wall and across the ceiling. (C1)
- Create a giant's castle in the role play corner using the giant food and other things that are over-sized. Find some over-sized clothes for dressing up. (C4)
- Make a collaborative picture of the giant using different materials such as fabric, corrugated card, buttons and shiny foil. (C5)

## ACTIVITY: Growing beans in jars

**Learning opportunity:** To help children discover how plants grow.

**Early Learning Goal:** Knowledge and Understanding of the World. Children will explore and recognise features of living things.

**Practical Pre-School**

**Resources:** Broad bean seeds; some large; clear glass jam-jars; blotting paper, paper towels.

**Organisation:** Small groups (each group has its own jar and bean).

**Key vocabulary:** Growing, strong, light, gravity, upright, sideways, germination, roots and shoots.

## WHAT TO DO:

Soak seeds before planting (preferably overnight).

Cut a piece of blotting paper to fit inside the jar. Push some crumpled paper towels into the middle of the jar. Push the soaked beans between the blotting paper and the outside of the jar. (You should be able to see the beans through the glass.) Place the seeds at different angles.

Keep the jars in a warm place out of direct sunlight. Keep the jars watered. Place some of the jars on their sides.

After a few days the roots and shoots should begin to appear. Ask children what grows first - the roots or the shoots? In which direction do they grow?

When the roots and shoots are a few centimetres long, turn some of the jars upside down. Ask children what they think will happen. Check in a few days if they are correct.

## ACTIVITY: Keeper of the Treasure

**Learning opportunity:** To help children work together and to increase their control and co-ordination.

**Early Learning Goal:** Physical Development: move confidently and imaginatively with increased control and co-ordination. Personal, Social and Emotional Development: work as part of a group.

**Resources:** A soft toy; a small bag of money (or something that could rattle); a small musical instrument.

**Organisation:** Whole group, a space big enough for the children to sit in a circle with room for moving in the middle of the circle.

**Key vocabulary:** Listening, creeping, crawling, quietly, silent.

## WHAT TO DO:

Sit children in a circle. Choose one child to sit in the middle and be the giant guarding his treasure.

Blindfold the giant and place his treasures near him: a soft toy (the chicken), some money in a bag (his gold), a small musical instrument (his harp).

Choose children from the circle to move quietly into the circle and take one of the treasures back to their place without being heard.

If the giant hears he or she must point in the direction of the sound. If the giant points in the right direction the treasure must be returned.

The game finishes when all three treasures have been rescued. A new giant is found and the game can continue.

## DISPLAY

Create a large beanstalk that goes up the wall and over the ceiling. A small castle can be placed at its end. Put the treasures on the high part of the beanstalk. Label leaves, stem and roots of the beanstalk.

On a table display the jars with the sprouting beans. Scribe the children's comments about their beans (they can write their name next to the comment) and place these near the jars.

# Week 5

# THE PRINCESS AND THE FROG

## PERSONAL, SOCIAL AND EMOTIONAL DEVELOPMENT

- Discuss the need to be sensitive to others feelings and the importance of keeping promises. (PS4, 5, 8)
- Discuss how you should look after pets and animals. (PS4)

## LANGUAGE AND LITERACY

- Read the story (by Jonathan Langley, Collins Lion Picture Books). As a group collect words that describe the princess. Write them on an outline of a princess. (L8, 16)
- Find other names that begin with I for Ivy and F for Frederick. (L11, 12)
- Find words that rhyme with ball. (L12, 18)

## MATHEMATICAL DEVELOPMENT

- Make ten paper frogs and ten lily pads. Put a hoop on a table to represent the pond. Place a different number of lily pads in the pond each time. Ask children to divide the frogs between the lily pads so no pad is empty. Help children to observe when there are the same number of frogs on each pad (for example, when there are five pads there will be two frogs on each) and when there are not (when there are three pads). (M5, 7)
- Give children plain paper frog shapes and ask them to decorate them with different patterns. (M8)
- Use mathematical language to describe the pond and the frog's journey to the castle. (M9, 10)
- Play the 'Princess and the Frog' fishing game (see activity opposite). (M4, 8, 9)

## KNOWLEDGE AND UNDERSTANDING OF THE WORLD

- Visit a local pond to see if there is any sign of frogspawn and tadpoles. If possible, take photographs. (K2, 9)
- Show children pictures of the life-cycle of a frog. Ask them to describe what is happening to the frog. (K4)
- Find a collection of round objects and see whether they float or sink in the water tray. (K4)

## PHYSICAL DEVELOPMENT

- Use pom-poms or bean bags to practise throwing and catching. (PD2)
- Set up different kinds of containers, such as waste bins, boxes, hoops, suitcases, so that children can practise throwing into a container. (PD8)

## CREATIVE DEVELOPMENT

- Use chalks on blue paper to make frogspawn and tadpole pictures based on the photographs taken at the local pond. Cover with cellophane to give a watery feel. Cut out strips of green paper and stick to the sides to edge the pond picture. (C1)
- Make up a frog jumping dance to jerky music. (C4)
- Cut out frogs from corrugated card and make rubbings to create interesting frog pictures. (C5)
- Make small frogs from green playdough and sit them on cardboard lily pads. (C5)
- Make pom-poms (see activity opposite). (C1)

## ACTIVITY: The Princess and the Frog fishing game

**Learning opportunity:** To help children sort by size and pattern.

**Early Learning Goal:** Mathematics. Compare, sort, match, order, sequence everyday objects.

**Resources:** A piece of card fastened into a circle; 20 picture cards with a paper fastener attached to the back; four magnet fishing rods.

**Organisation:** Small groups of two to four children.

**Key vocabulary:** Big, little, large, small, striped, spotted.

## WHAT TO DO:

Make 20 'golden balls': four large and spotted, four large and striped, four small and spotted, four small and striped and four plain yellow.

Cut an A2 piece of white card in half lengthways. Join up the ends and fasten to make the pond.

Place all the 'golden balls' in the pond for the children to try to catch.

The winner is the child with the most sets of balls.

## ACTIVITY: Making large pom-poms

**Learning opportunity:** Children will discover the use of different materials.

**Early Learning Goal:** Creative Development. Explore texture and colour, shape and form, using a widening range of materials.

**Resources:** Strong, large cardboard rings with a hole in the middle; wool in various thickness and colours of yellow.

**Organisation:** Small groups with an adult helper.

**Key vocabulary:** Circle, wool, thick, thin, fold, wrap.

## WHAT TO DO:

Cut two 20cm diameter circles from strong card for each pom-pom. Cut out a 10cm diameter circle in the middle of each larger circle.

Join the first piece of wool around inside through the hole then ask children to keep wrapping wool of different thickness and colours through the hole and around the outside until the centre hole is full.

An adult cuts the wool between the two circles and wraps either string or a strong piece of wool around the cut pieces and between the two circles. Secure the string or wool and leave a long piece as a hanger if needed.

The pom-poms can be used as decorations or for ball games. Experiment with different sized circles.

Variation: Make green pom-poms and stick eyes onto them to make frogs.

## DISPLAY

Make a display of the life-cycle of a frog and write the children's explanations of what is happening to label the pictures. Display the photographs of your visit to a pond alongside the children's frogspawn and tadpole pictures. Put the playdough frogs and cardboard lily-pads on a table covered with a blue cloth or blue paper with the pom-pom frogs.

# Week 6
## ONCE UPON A TIME

### PERSONAL, SOCIAL AND EMOTIONAL DEVELOPMENT

- Discuss how we should treat each other, for example, keep our promises, not say unkind things, not take other people's things. Ask them to remember in which stories did someone not keep their promise, was unkind to someone else, stole somebody else's things. (PS4, 9)
- Encourage a 'being friendly' week. (PS7)
- Have a 'fairy tale' circle time (see activity opposite). (PS13)

### LANGUAGE AND LITERACY

- Ask children to retell a favourite story from the last few weeks. (L9)
- Find some more stories about princes and princesses and read them to the group - some suggestions are on the Resources page 21. (L14)
- Find more than one version of a story such as 'Little Red Riding Hood'. Ask children how they are different. (L14)
- Talk about the things that happen in fairy stories. Make a list of some of the characters found in the stories. (L9, 14)
- Look at the opening words in fairy stories - do they always begin with 'Once upon a time'? do they always finish with 'they lived happily ever after'? (L8 14)
- Create a story together (see activity opposite). (L3, 4, 9)

### MATHEMATICAL DEVELOPMENT

- Make a survey of favourite stories and make a block chart showing who likes what. Use the outcome for counting practice. (M2, 5)
- Use finger puppets of fairy story characters to illustrate number finger rhymes like 'Five Little Speckled Frogs'. (M1, 2)
- Adapt 'One elephant went out to play' to 'One giant went out to play'. (M1, 2)

### KNOWLEDGE AND UNDERSTANDING OF THE WORLD

- Make a map of a journey taken by a favourite fairy tale character. (K9, 11)
- Talk about places in fairy stories. Discuss how the environments in fairy stories are different from where the children live. (K11)

### PHYSICAL DEVELOPMENT

- Create a simple obstacle course for children to take a pretend journey in a fairy tale land. (PD6)

### CREATIVE DEVELOPMENT

- Dance and sing 'There was a Princess Long Ago'. (C2, 4)
- Make half-masks of favourite fairy tale characters. (C4, 5)
- Make stick puppets for 'Little Red Riding Hood' or 'Goldilocks and the Three Bears'. (C4, 5)

### ACTIVITY: An interactive story

**Learning opportunity:** Developing children's use of vocabulary and imaginative response.

**Early Learning Goal:** Language and Literacy. Children will use a growing vocabulary to express thoughts and use familiar words to communicate meaning; listen and respond to stories.

**Resources:** None.

**Organisation:** Whole group with adult helpers in a space large enough to move around in.

**Key vocabulary:** Will be developed by the story.

### WHAT TO DO:

Create a space that has boundaries either by using chairs or by placing ropes in a large rectangle.

Gather children inside the rectangle in a sitting circle.

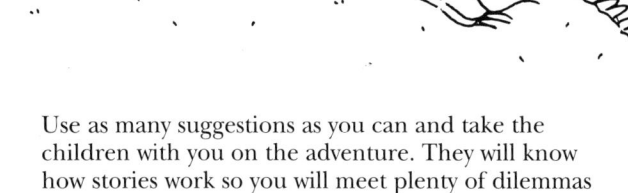

Explain they are going to tell a story with you and the story can only happen inside the rectangle. They are going to be part of the story and not just listening to one. Remind them about working together and listening carefully to what people are saying.

Tell them you will begin the story but, as it is going to be their story as well, they will need to listen because you are going to ask them what should happen next.

Begin the story by saying you are a prince who is looking for a beautiful princess. The prince has been told she lives in this area but he does not know where. He has also heard there may be a giant who lives nearby. Ask the children what they know about the princess and the giant.

From this point let the children tell the story. It is very tempting for the adults to take over! Listen carefully to what the children say and play out the actions they suggest. They may, for example, tell you:

- she lives in a palace in the forest
- she is asleep
- she has a wicked step-mother
- you can only get there by night
- there are lots of wolves in the forest

Use as many suggestions as you can and take the children with you on the adventure. They will know how stories work so you will meet plenty of dilemmas and difficult situations which you will all have to solve.

## ACTIVITY: Fairy tale circle time

**Learning opportunity:** To allow children to discuss difficult problems in role.

**Early Learning Goal:** Personal, Social and Emotional Development. Children will learn to be sensitive to the needs of others and show respect for people of other cultures and beliefs.

**Resources:** A half-mask of favourite fairy tale character.

**Organisation:** Whole group or half a group.

**Key vocabulary:** Kind, unkind, cruel, gentle, good, bad, promise, responsibility.

## WHAT TO DO:

Gather children into a sitting circle and ask them to put on their masks. Ask each character to say who they are.

Pass around a 'golden ball' and each character says what they have done to help someone that week and something they have done that is naughty.

Talk about the good and bad things the different fairy story characters have done.

Discuss ways of making bad things good again. Ask how some of the fairy story characters did it.

## DISPLAY

Make a book display of all the fairy stories used in the topic and others. Try to have more than one version of the same story for children to look at.

# BRINGING IT ALL TOGETHER

## A FAIRY STORY BOOK DAY

Explain to the children that at the end of the week they are going to have a fairy story book day. This is something that everyone can help to prepare. Everyone, including the adults, will come dressed up as a character from a fairy tale. Encourage them to ask for help at home with their costume. There may be some parents or grandparents who like sewing or making things who would help.

## DECORATING THE ROOM

Talk about how your setting can be changed into different fairy story environments. Make an enchanted castle or a magic wood - trees with faces painted on can be hung round the walls.

Silhouettes of fairy story characters can be cut out of paper and fixed to the walls.

Make different characters into paper dancing dolls which can be joined together to make paper chains across the room.

Mobiles of clouds and stars can be hung from the ceiling.

## INVITATIONS

Who is going to be invited? Each child can design and make a card to invite their parent, carer, friend to the afternoon of your fairy story book day.

## OTHER INVITATIONS

If they are given enough notice, the local library and the local bookseller may come in with a display of books to borrow or to buy.

During the afternoon you can arrange:

- displays of children's work
- displays of fairy story books
- a fancy dress parade of all the characters
- puppet shows of favourite stories put on by the children for their parents
- children can help to teach their parents some of the rhymes and songs they have learned. This could end with everyone joining in 'There was a princess long ago'.

# RESOURCES

## RESOURCES TO COLLECT:

- Magazines and catalogues with pictures of shoes.
- Collection of seeds.
- Baking materials and ingredients (see recipes).
- Pictures of the life-cycle of the frog.
- Broad bean seeds, jam-jars.
- Collection of fairy stories.
- Wools in different colours of yellow.
- Collection of mirrors.
- Magnets.

## EVERYDAY RESOURCES:

- Boxes, large and small for modelling.
- Papers and cards of different weights, colours and textures, for example, sugar, corrugated card, silver and shiny papers.
- Dry powder paints for mixing and mixed paints for covering large areas such as card tree trunks.
- Different sized paint brushes from household brushes to thin brushes for delicate work and a variety of paint mixing containers.
- A variety of drawing and colouring pencils, crayons, pastels, charcoals, chalks.
- Additional decorative and finishing materials such as sequins, foils, glitter, tinsel, shiny wool and threads, beads, pieces of textiles, parcel ribbon.
- Table covers.

## FAIRY STORY BOOKS

Individual stories:

*The Gingerbread Man* by J A Rowe (North-South Paperbacks).

*The Elves and The Shoemaker* by F Hunia (*Read It Yourself* Ladybird).

*Snow White and the Seven Dwarfs* by J Koralek (Macdonald Young Books).

*Jack and the Beanstalk* by J Poole (Macdonald Young Books).

*The Princess and the Frog* by J Langley (Collins Lion Picture Books).

Collections of fairy stories are published by many of the leading children's publishers.

Other well-known fairy stories not used in the topic:

- *Sleeping Beauty*
- *Goldilocks and the Three Bears*
- *The Three Little Pigs*
- *The Enormous Turnip*
- *Rumpelstiltskin*
- *Rapunzel*
- *Little Red Riding Hood*
- *The Adventures of Tom Thumb*
- *The Ugly Duckling*
- *Cinderella*
- *The Three Billy Goats Gruff*
- *Town Mouse and Country Mouse*
- *Little Red Hen*
- *The Princess and the Pea*
- *The Hare and the Tortoise*

## POEMS AND SONGS

*This Little Puffin* by Elizabeth Matterson (Puffin).

*Out and About* by Shirley Hughes (Walker).

*Over and Over Again: Poems and songs for the very young* by Barbara Ireson and Christopher Rowe (Beaver Books).

# COLLECTING EVIDENCE OF CHILDREN'S LEARNING

Monitoring children's development is an important task. Keeping a record of children's achievements will help you to see progress and will draw attention to those who are having difficulties for some reason. If a child needs additional professional help, such as speech therapy, your records will provide valuable evidence.

Records should be the result of collaboration between group leaders, parents and carers. Parents should be made aware of your record keeping policies when their child joins your group. Show them the type of records you are keeping and make sure they understand that they have an opportunity to contribute. As a general rule, your records should form an open document. Any parent should have access to records relating to his or her child. Take regular opportunities to talk to parents about children's progress. If you have formal discussions regarding children about whom you have particular concerns, a dated record of the main points should be kept.

## KEEPING IT MANAGEABLE

Records should be helpful in informing group leaders, adult helpers and parents and always be for the benefit of the child. However, keeping records of every aspect of each child's development can become a difficult task. The sample shown will help to keep records manageable and useful. The golden rule is to keep them simple.

Observations will basically fall into three categories:

- **Spontaneous records:**

Sometimes you will want to make a note of observations as they happen, for example, a child is heard counting cars accurately during a play activity, or is seen to play collaboratively for the first time.

- **Planned observations:**

Sometimes you will plan to make observations of children's developing skills in their everyday activities. Using the learning opportunity identified for an activity will help you to make appropriate judgements about children's capabilities and to record them systematically.

To collect information:

- talk to children about their activities and listen to their responses;
- listen to children talking to each other;
- observe children's work such as early writing, drawings, paintings and 3D models. (Keeping photocopies or photographs is sometimes useful.)

Sometimes you may wish to set up 'one off' activities for the purposes of monitoring development. Some groups, for example, ask children to make a drawing of themselves at the beginning of each term to record their progressing skills in both co-ordination and observation. Do not attempt to make records following every activity!

- **Reflective observations:**

It is useful to spend regular time reflecting on the progress of a few children (about four each week). Aim to make some brief comments about each child every half term.

## INFORMING YOUR PLANNING

Collecting evidence about children's progress is time consuming and it is important that it is useful.

When you are planning, use the information you have collected to help you to decide what learning opportunities you need to provide next for children. For example, a child who has poor pencil or brush control will benefit from more play with dough or construction toys to build the strength of hand muscles.

## Example of recording chart

| Name: Lucy Copson | | D.O.B. 26.2.97 | | Date of entry: 13.9.00 | |
|---|---|---|---|---|---|
| **Term** | Personal, Social and Emotional | Language and Literacy | Mathematical Development | Knowledge and Understanding | Physical Development | Creative Development |
| **ONE** | Reluctant to say good bye to mother. Prefers adult company 20.9.00 EMH | Enjoying listening to stories, particularly 'The Princess and the Frog' 20.11.00 EMH | Is able to say numbers to ten and to count accurately five objects. Recognises and names squares and circles. 5.11.00 BM | Enjoyed growing beans in a jar. 16.10.00 AC | Can balance on one leg. Finds cutting difficult. 16.10.00 AC | Enjoys music. Joins in well with singing. 20.10.00 LSS |
| **TWO** | | | | | | |
| **THREE** | | | | | | |

# SKILLS OVERVIEW OF SIX-WEEK PLAN

| Week | Topic focus | Personal, Social and Emotional Development | Language and Literacy | Mathematical Development | Knowledge and Understanding of the World | Physical Development | Creative Development |
|---|---|---|---|---|---|---|---|
| 1 | The Gingerbread Man | Developing awareness of personal hygiene | Listening Repeating from memory | Weighing Comparison | Discussion of environment | Developing gross motor control | Use of materials Response to music |
| 2 | The Elves and the Shoemaker | Helping others | Developing individual vocabulary | Sorting Matching | Develop sense of past and present | Developing use of space | Observation Creativity |
| 3 | Snow White and the Seven Dwarfs | Share feelings and ideas with others | Recognise own name | Symmetry Patterns | Questioning Investigation | Handling materials appropriately | Use of imagination Painting |
| 4 | Jack and the Beanstalk | Making choices | Describing Comprehension | Counting Problem solving | Exploring the living world | Moving with increased control | Exploring materials |
| 5 | The Princess and the Frog | Keeping promises Responsibility | Describing Writing | Grouping Use of maths language | Floating and sinking | Throwing and catching | Working in 3D |
| 6 | Once upon a time | Good and bad behaviour Sharing | Storytelling | Simple block graphs | Making maps | Moving with control and concentration | Exploring materials through mask and puppet making |

Practical Pre-School

Planning for Learning through Fairy Stories 23

# HOME LINKS

The theme of Fairy Stories lends itself to useful links with children's homes and families. Through working together children and adults gain respect for each other and build comfortable and confident relationships.

staff are willing to come into schools and playgroups. There are also theatre groups who perform favourite tales in school settings.

## RESOURCE REQUESTS

- Ask to borrow biscuit cutters for making the gingerbread men.
- Ask for contributions of old shoes with interesting patterns on the sole.

## PREPARING THE FAIRY TALE BOOK DAY

- Invite parents, carers and friends to help decorate parts of the school or playgroup with pictures, 3-D mobiles and hangings to create different fairy story environments.
- Encourage parents to help prepare a costume for the fairy tale day for their children and themselves.

## ESTABLISHING PARTNERSHIPS

- Keep parents informed about the topic of Fairy Stories, and the stories and themes for each week. By understanding the work of the group, parents will enjoy the involvement of contributing ideas, time and resources.
- Request parental permission before taking children out to visit a pond. Describe your route and the purposes of the activity. Additional parental help will be necessary for this activity to be carried out safely.
- Photocopy the parent's page for each child to take home.
- Invite carers, friends, childminders and families to share the Fairy Story Book Day at the end of the topic.

## VISITING STORYTELLERS

- Invite a parent, carer or friend who is willing to share a favourite fairy story to come and either read or tell the story to the group.
- If funds are available, invite in a professional storyteller to create new fairy stories with the children. Sometimes members of the local library